Excited About
ENERGY

by Nadia Higgins

illustrations by Andrés Martínez Ricci

Content Consultant:

Paul Ohmann, PhD · Associate Professor of Physics · University of St. Thomas

visit us at www.abdopublishing.com

Published by Magic Wagon, a division of the ABDO Publishing Group, 8000 West 78th Street, Edina, Minnesota 55439. Copyright © 2009 by Abdo Consulting Group, Inc. International copyrights reserved in all countries. All rights reserved. No part of this book may be reproduced in any form without written permission from the publisher.

Looking Glass Library™ is a trademark and logo of Magic Wagon.

Printed in the United States.

Text by Nadia Higgins
Illustrations by Andrés Martínez Ricci
Edited by Jill Sherman
Interior layout and design by Nicole Brecke
Cover design by Nicole Brecke

Library of Congress Cataloging-in-Publication Data

Higgins, Nadia.
 Excited about energy / by Nadia Higgins ; illustrated by Andrés Martínez Ricci ; content consultant, Paul Ohmann.
    p. cm. — (Science rocks!)
 Includes index.
 ISBN 978-1-60270-277-6
 1. Power resources—Juvenile literature. I. Martínez Ricci, Andrés. II. Ohmann, Paul. III. Title.
 TJ163.23.H54 2008
 531'.6—dc22
                        2008001636

Table of Contents

Energy Gets Things Going 4

Types of Energy 6

Changing Energy 12

Energy High and Low 15

The Sun 18

Kinds of Fuel 22

Activity 30

Fun Facts 31

Glossary 32

On the Web 32

Index 32

Energy Gets Things Going

What do a banana, a bus, and your body have in common?

They're all full of energy! Energy is what gets things going.

Types of Energy

You twirl. You tumble. Motion is a form of energy.

Keep on exercising and you'll get hot. Heat is energy, too.

Your body uses energy to sleep and think. It takes energy for you to read this book.

Vroom. As a bus zips down the street, it rumbles. Sound is another kind of energy.

The bus turns on its headlights. That's right! Light is energy, too.

But what about that banana? It doesn't move. It's not hot, loud, or bright.

That banana has potential energy stored inside it. When you eat the banana, its energy goes into your body.

Changing Energy

Energy can move from one thing to another. As it does, it often changes form.

The banana's energy lets you tap and twirl. Potential energy in the banana changes to motion in your body.

A battery stores potential energy. The potential energy changes to electrical energy when the battery is used.

Energy High and Low

Another kind of potential energy can come just from putting something up high.

Climb up a diving board. Up there, your body has a lot of potential energy. It just takes a nudge for you to fall and make a huge splash.

15

Now you're standing in the shallow end of the pool. Your body doesn't have potential energy anymore. You'd have to work really hard to make a splash that big!

17

The Sun

You get energy from bananas and other food. But where does food's energy come from?

It comes from the sun. The sun is the source of almost all energy on Earth.

The sun gives off heat. Plants use the sun's energy to grow. They store the energy in their leaves and fruit.

When animals eat plants, the energy transfers to the animals' bodies. When you eat plants and animals, the energy goes into your body.

Kinds of Fuel

Chop up wood and make a campfire.

Plants can be used as fuel. Burning fuel provides us with energy.

Until the late 1800s, Americans used wood to do all their cooking. Woodstoves heated their homes.

Millions of years ago, giant plants soaked up the sun's energy. The plants fed ancient sea creatures.

Little by little, those plants turned into coal. The sea creatures turned into oil and natural gas.

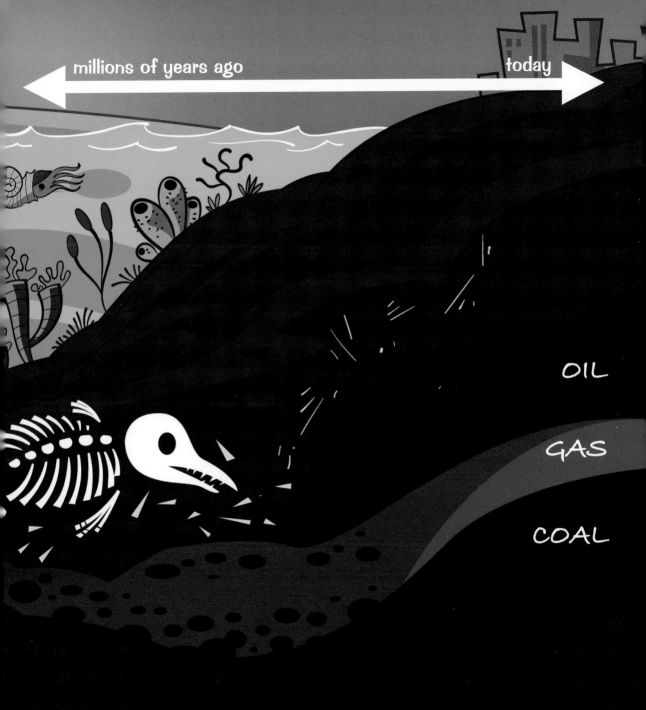

Coal, oil, and natural gas are fossil fuels. Fossil fuels heat our homes. They power our cars and give us electricity.

But Earth's fossil fuels are running out!

You can help save fossil fuels by using less energy. Turn down the heat. Turn off lights.

Scientists are looking for new ways to run cars and heat homes. Sunlight, wind, and even ocean waves are energy sources that will never run out.

Energy makes our world shine, move, and grow. Are you excited about energy?

Activity

Demolition Day

What you need:

A deck of cards, blocks, or dominoes

A hair dryer

A pot lid

A big spoon (or anything else good for banging)

What to do:

1. Make a house of cards or a block tower. If you have dominoes, line them up so they are standing in a row.

2. How many ways can you knock over your creation? You can nudge it with you finger. In that case, energy is transferred from your body to the structure. Now try stomping or shouting. Do those work? What other ways can energy from your body knock down your structure?

3. With an adult's help, turn on the hair dryer and aim it at your creation. Does that knock it down? How is energy changing form now?

4. Try banging on the pot lid with the spoon. Does that work? What other ways can you use energy to knock down your structure?

Fun Facts

Fuel gets used up, but energy never goes away. As the fuel burns, the energy in the fuel changes into heat, light, motion, and other forms of energy. Energy can keep changing form forever, but it will never disappear.

In the early 1900s, 26 million horses and mules lived in the United States. They pulled farm equipment and hauled carts. They did work that is now done by machines powered by fossil fuels. Today, 80 percent of energy in the United States comes from fossil fuels.

In 2006, a typical U.S. family spent $1,500 on that year's energy bills.

Only 10 percent of energy that goes into a traditional lightbulb makes light. The rest of it is wasted as heat. New energy-efficient lightbulbs give off much less heat.

Where does the sun get its energy? A gas called hydrogen fuels the sun. Nuclear reactions inside the hydrogen atoms give off enormous amounts of energy. The sun has enough hydrogen to last about another 5 billion years!

Energy is measured in a unit called a joule. A joule is the amount of energy it takes to lift a one-pound (.45 kg) object that is nine inches (23 cm) high. A piece of toast with butter has about 300,000 joules stored inside it.

Some small lighthouses are powered by electricity made from ocean waves.

Glossary

fossil fuel—coal, oil, or natural gas that came from ancient plants or sea creatures.

fuel—something that can be used to create energy.

natural gas—a kind of fossil fuel that comes from nature.

potential energy—energy stored inside something.

transfer—to go from one thing into another.

On the Web

To learn more about energy, visit ABDO Publishing Company on the World Wide Web at **www.abdopublishing.com**. Web sites about energy are featured on our Book Links page. These links are routinely monitored and updated to provide the most current information available.

Index

animals 21, 24

banana 4, 11, 12, 18

batteries 12

body 4, 6, 10, 11, 12, 15, 16, 21

bus 4, 8

cars 26, 28

coal 24, 26

Earth 18, 26

eat 11, 21

elastic 17

electrical energy . . . 12, 26

exercise 6

fat 10

fossil fuel 26, 27

fuel 22

grow 20, 28

heat 6, 20, 26, 27, 28

light 8, 27

motion 6, 12

natural gas 24, 26

oil 24, 26

plants 20, 21, 22, 24

potential energy . . . 11, 12, 15, 16, 17

sound 8

sun 18, 20, 24, 28

waves 28

wind 28